Winter Solstice

Reflections on Light
and Darkness
in a Season of Grace

By
Father Kenneth E. Lasch

CATHOLIC BOOK PUBLISHING CORP.
New Jersey

Dedication

**To my parents, Gabe and Irene
and to my sister, Carol
who made the gift of hope
their theme for life.**

**Special gratitude to Mary Aktay
whose insistent encouragement led to
the publication of this little 'tome.'**

Artwork created in PhotoFunia from photos of M. Aktay, K. E. Lasch and Creative Commons on Pixabay.com

The cover art is Father Lasch's rendering of the cover of Corpus magazine. With acknowledgment to the original artist who is unknown.

(T-940)

ISBN 978-1-947070-36-3

© 2019 by Catholic Book Publishing Corp.
77 West End Rd.
Totowa, NJ 07512
Printed in Canada
www.catholicbookpublishing.com

Contents

Preface

The somber days of November give
way to Advent
with the songs of congregants
waiting the dawn of a new day of grace
and opportunity.
It's the grace of the season
And Jesus is the reason for the season,

God's embrace of humanity is total;
how else could God have become
incarnate?
But Christmas is just the beginning of a
love story
that continues to unfold
day by day in you and me.

There's nothing wrong with Christmas
cheer
and festive celebrations
as long as we retain a collective memory
of Jesus' birth, not just back to this unique
event
but to the memory of Jesus in his many
'comings' throughout the ages,
the memory that helps us to become
conduits of grace and mercy today.

Season of Adventure
An Advent Meditation

If you rise early
and look to the east on a clear winter
    day,
the sky is a faint blue—the color of dawn.
The earth seems to respect this time of
    day
and offers a calm respite
before the noise of trucks and busses
    begin.
Somehow, the morning brings hope
even to the restless sleeper.
The sailor is glad to see the dawn
and the night watchman knows that rest
    is near.

Blue is the color of Advent
but we await not the sun but the Son,
and the world is not quite as respectful
    of the earth.
There is hardly a calm
except that before the storm.

There is so much to do and
so little time in which to do it.
Do what?
Go to work, go to school;
Invest time, make money, build a church
    or a tower of Babel?
Make a list, shop for gifts, trim a tree.
Blue for hope or blue for the blues?

"A voice cries out in the desert:
'Make ready the way of the Lord, clear
    Him a straight path.'"

How can we hear His voice
Unless we, like the earth, respect the
    dawn of His coming
with calm.
Take time.
Take a breath.
Be at peace.

All will be well.

The Grace of Advent

Searching and seeking
for knowledge, understanding and
    wisdom?
No! for peace and serenity.
Are they not the same—wisdom the
    path to serenity?
Searching and seeking
a fuller experience
of life
of God
Knowing many things
never enough;
touching the surface
unable to comprehend the mystery
"beneath the tip of the iceberg"
Dreaming
of knowing more
beyond the rational,
of knowing myself
as God knows me—
soul deep
where freedom begins,
where freedom reigns.

"Free to be faithful"
Faithful to what
to whom?
To code and custom?
law and life-style
structure, stability or status?
Such faithfulness is shallow
detached from the soul;
stagnant separated from risk.
Leave home; gone searching,
"gone fishing"
looking in, looking out, looking all
    around.
going out to play
with God!
New vision, new wisdom__
left brain meeting the right brain;
senex and *puer* play together
in the field of experience.
Animus and anima exult in the reverie
    of myth__
explored,
energy harnessed,
creativity unleashed,
hard nosed compassion discovered,

no—uncovered.
Community emerges
commitment established.
Via positiva, the way of the pilgrim
and poet,
artist,
preacher.
Jesus—composer, poet, sculptor, artist.
The search is never over.
New digs for now—
Forever?
Who knows?
The universe is a billion years old
or more?
Back to origins—
original blessing:
"I am the alpha and the omega,
the beginning and the end."
God within and all around.
Uncreated love,
gift of love,
"I will pour out my spirit on women and
    men—
old and young"
on every creature in the sea, on land and
    in the air.

Gratitude to family, friends and neighbors –
co-searchers and seekers, conduits of
    grace
who provide the time and space for the
    search.
Love for you who model the search,
you searchers and seekers
keeping hope alive—
No pain, no gain;
letting go of yesterday.
Happy days ahead;
the best is yet to come!
Hold fast to the dream.

Season of Seeking
Quantum Leap

As I write this we are fast approaching
the winter solstice
with its premonition of end times.
But searchers and seekers of God,
people of faith in what cannot be seen,
do not deny the glory of nature
with its ever recurring cycle of birth,
death and rebirth.
Surely we can make of winter a liturgy
with its call to silence—
the sacred sounds of nature's song at
daylight,
the holy proclamation of life in the face
of death
then the silent sunset to accompany
evening prayer
and the starlit night to keep at bay
the fear of darkness and death.

Creation is a cathedral not made by
human hands,
fashioned by the Artist of endless ages—
'Ancient of Days.'

The God of heaven and earth was not
    content to hoard this blessed beauty
but deigned to share it with earthly
    creatures—
women and men, who at their very best,
reflect a Mother's wisdom and the
    generosity of a 'prodigal' father,
giving ample testimony to the never-
    ending love of this generous God.
People of faith living in the rhythm of
    God's life.
They smell God's breath in the air
and they feel the beat of God's heart
    deep within their own hearts.

How can we not give praise?
If we keep silent, "the very stones will
    cry out!"

Christmas, celebrated appropriately in
    the northern hemisphere
shortly after the winter solstice,
is the anchor feast of Christendom—
    incarnation.
It is the commemoration of a singular
    event

that touched the core of humanity as did
no other event in history
except creation
when God breathed into the void and
gave birth to the universe.
Some folks still debate the origin of the
universe:
creationists who argue for the origin of
the world in seven days,
and "evolutionists" who insist on a more
gradual
progression from the 'big bang.'
But the debate will be won not by
scientists or scientologists
and not even by theologians,
but by artists and poets.
The explorations of scientists and
theologians
are not useless or without merit—
every quantum leap of understanding is
a step closer to the origin of life.
The artist and the poet however, see the
hand of God in all creation,
the mind of God in every act of nature
and they feel the heartbeat of God in
every creature.

Winter Solstice —
Timeless Encounter

Refined silk sky,
alabaster window shielding eternity,
shades of pink and gray with amber here
    and there.
Clouds painted with broad brush
    strokes
blending with the distant sky
barely distinguished one from another,
a veritable talisman.

Quiet air.

Tired sun makes its brief appearance at
    the eastern edge
only to hasten its descent toward the
    'south gate,'
scarcely touching the western edge
    before sinking into the distant
    meadow.
Silhouetted trees create long shadows
    traversing the earth.
Barren branches and naked stalks bravely
    face north
braced for the long, cold night.

Silent night.

Winter Solstice
preparing for a holy night—
The Holy Night.

Nature demands our attention
to a place in time and space
where earth and heaven met for one
brief moment.
God and humanity conjoined in eternal
embrace.
Timeless encounter;
endless mercy;
God with skin.
Evil confounded by compassion,
darkness no longer in control.
Eternal light—
bright promise of eternal life.

Fallow time remains, not to be wasted.
Pay attention to the stars.
Remain silent.
Stay alert for the prophet's call—
angelic voices
and shepherds' songs.

Every year the same words
But never the same message
Endings and new beginnings
Again as if for the first time.

Put to rest the pain and sorrow of other
    times
and other places
as if they never existed;
hold instead
to cherished memories of good times,
life-giving moments of gladness
when the songs of our hearts
replaced the bitter taste of harsh words.

No theology can match the sacred myth
    of the poet's verse
Nor expose the incomprehensible mys-
    tery of the divine absence
that makes present the eternal longing
    for ultimate resolution
supernatural no longer super
but a continuum of the natural flowing
    into the vast universe
where humanity lives comfortably with
    its divine origin:
original blessing.

Differences dissolved,
virtue expanding on the beauty of the
    Godself
faith, hope and love fulfilled.

No tainted skies or painted thoughts;
No broken branches or shattered
    dreams
Nothing between us and God
And all those we have loved so dearly in
    life and in death.
The Christ Event has made the vision
    possible.

A brief respite in time
with lasting impressions for believers
and still hidden messages for people of
    goodwill everywhere.
God's breath is in the air
and in the Season.

Come Lord Jesus, come!

Season of Peace
The Gift of Peace

Through the maze of history
the figure emerges
unfettered,
bound only by love.

Timeless but timely,
centuries old,
but childlike.

In word, clear.
In deed, strong.
Neither staff nor sandal,
no sword or spear.
Giver of truth, gift of peace.
"Where do you live?"
"Come and see."

Life lost, love returned.
Lamb of God.
"Come, follow me."

His life is never over,
his birth is ever new
in you,
in me.

"Come and see.
Come, follow me."

Ties that Blind

There is a yearning
in the heart of even the most estranged
      from God
or friend or spouse—
a longing for peace and wholeness.
There is, in this season of grace
an opportunity for such,
but you must first un-grasp
that which binds you to earth
and remove
the blindness
that prevents you from seeing in God—
a friend, your friend.

Be at peace in Christ
who grasped at nothing,
and gained all for love.

Season of Hope
Want Ad

Help wanted
Hope needed.
Mixed signals, mixed messages—
Confusion all around.
The people plead for peace
and cry, "Shoot to kill!"
Where will it all end?

Throw away children,
abused women,
homeless men—
helpless all.

A lone voice is heard
from the depth of all ages:
like a whisper in the heart,
a song of love.

A lamp is lit from a distant star,
a spark in the eye of a child.
Night turns to dawn.

Jesus is coming again.
Help is on the way.
Hope is still alive!

Only a Crack in the Wall

...But wide enough for eyes to pierce
through decades of darkness.
Hope restored, hearts renewed, hands
rejoined;
east meets west at dawn.

"Justice shall flourish in his time,
and fullness of peace forever."

(Psalm 72:12-13)

Christmas is about east meeting west,
north meeting south,
and God entering history through the
human heart.
It's about erasing hurt, restoring hope
and giving love.

May Jesus be in your heart and in your
household
and may you be blessed with peace now
and in the coming year.

Don't Miss the Point

It was said that his coming was imminent.
Some people still believe it,
but live with the hope that his coming is
    a long way off.
Meanwhile, they busy themselves with
    "stuff"
that keeps them safe from personal hurt.
They work for power and position
in the pursuit of wealth
with the hope that it will protect them
from the imprisonment of poverty
and make them truly free.

But they miss the point.

Jesus is immanent and is eminently
    simple.
He appears wherever and whenever
    people embrace one another
in the pursuit of justice, integrity and
    peace
and in the recognition that we are all
    equal—

sisters and brothers created in the image and likeness of God.

May Christmas bring you the consolation that you are loved by God forever.

Season of Expectation
Election Day

His reputation preceded him
prior to his arrival in Jerusalem
in time for election day.
To many, he was an unknown entity;
after all, "What good could come out of
   Nazareth?"

The Democrats were thinking
about adopting him as a candidate.
He seemed to speak their language:
new deal, social reform, outreach to the
   poor.

The Republicans also considered his
   candidacy
because he spoke of family values
and personal responsibility.

The liberals in both parties liked him
   because
he challenged the status quo.

The Conservatives found him appealing
because he said he would not do away
   with the law,
"...not even the smallest letter of the
   law..."

Everyone cheered him when he arrived,
waving flags and shouting, "He's our
   man!"
He was invited to several talk shows
and to many pulpits too.
But he kept on saying,
"My kingdom is not of this world!"

But they all missed the point.
The day before elections
he was condemned and crucified.

People still miss the point.
I hope someday we'll all get the point.

May the grace of Christmas
enlighten you and me
that we may be a light to all
who search for wisdom
and strive for integrity.

The Heartbeat of God

The preacher said:
"The world is hungry for God!"
Indeed,
but it does not acknowledge
or even recognize its hunger.

Is it denial, doubt or despair,
which blinds the "believer?"
Or is it the glow of worldly lights
which challenge the Light
that came into the world?—
The true light,
that enlightens everyone."

(John 1:10)

Jesus is the one
who reminds us once more
that we are created in the image and
   likeness of God.

Jesus is the one
who enables us to acknowledge our
   hunger for God.

Jesus is the one
who enables us to hear and feel
the "heartbeat of God."

God's heart
will never stop beating
for God can never stop being God.

"No one has ever seen God.
It is God the only Son,
who is close to the Father's heart,
who made Him known." (John 1:18)

Blessed are those who enable others
to hear the heartbeat of God
in the wilderness,
in the city;
in Asia, Africa, and America-north, south
    and central;
in Bagdad, Beijing, and Bosnia—
in the depths of humanity everywhere.

May you hear the heartbeat of God
    during this season and in every
    season.

Season of Contradiction
No More Merry Christmas

In the midst of tinsel and merriment,
the poet said, "Post Christendom has
    arrived!"
the signs are all around us:
No more "Merry Christmas";
"Happy Holidays," instead.
Children laughing at the sacred.
Doctors of death
devouring the human spirit
when it is most open to help and hope
and life.
Toys and games for the poor
soothing the conscience of the rich,
filling the coffers of consumer madness
and skewing the global economy.

But there are signs too
That Christ is still here,
Alive and well.
The signs of the poet
Are the signs of contradiction
About which Jesus has spoken many
    times

And our consciousness of them
Is but an indication of the potential
For goodness and generosity that is in
    all of us
Despite our proneness to selfishness
    and sin.

So let the grace of the season
take hold within our hearts
and let the Son of Justice
take root in our lives.
The Christ story is far from over
and the mystery will continue
to bring down the mighty
and lift up the lowly.

PEACE ON EARTH

The Time Clock

Age pressed on the weary clock,
its hands tired from making rounds
in the chambers of time—a timely
    reminder:
how quickly we must surrender
to seasons salted with the smell of
    eternal winds.

Long shadows mark the length of days
too short for merriment
waiting for a better time to play.

Earth absorbs the pain of progress
hungering for life;
rivers thirst for fresh streams
making their way toward rusty seas.

Trumpeted towers of gilted steel stand
    mute
over barrios, barricades and borders that
    speak
a different language—
street language.

Life on the periphery
outside the margins of time
held hostage in field hospitals of mud
    and mortar
waiting for the embrace of caring
    mothers

Young men and women of every color,
    creed and gender
march to the beat of different drums.

Time marches on!

Where are the angels of mercy?
Heralds of good news: the end is just
    the beginning.
Play me a song, say the crowds to the
    soothsayers.
Let the sages have their day.
Wisdom!
Let us be attentive to the strains of
    yesterday.
Oh that we had listened.
to the weary prophets;
and attended to the signs of the times,
but time marches on!

Tucked away in the depth of time
the prayers of an ancient spring in the
    midst of winter,
choirs of winged creatures
chant songs of welcome.

Put away the clock, no time check
    necessary

A new day is dawning __
a timely reminder that
winter is not to last forever

Against the dark silky sky,
long shadows bow before the ancient
    star
whose light will not be quenched
until all humanity stands tall in its
    radiance.

Season of Mystery
Quiet Love

When I was a child
I used to think of God as an old man
high in the sky
with a long white beard stretching over
   the earth,
sweeping silk silver-lined clouds.
A sort of Santa Claus—
a gentle soul but not adverse to "making
   a list and checking it twice
to find out who's naughty or nice."
Such talk among adults is silly isn't it?
Fodder for Gnostics or agnostics and
   even atheists?
Perhaps, but I think God enjoys a bit of
   banter now and then.
And I suspect that God is often amused
at the attempts of great and small,
of prophets, priests and popes among
   them
to pin on God a personality
as if such were possible

though I do believe artists and poets
    have come close
in their playful pursuit to depict
the movement of love through the lens
    of ancient sages
down through the ages…

Quiet love.
'The Great Mystery"
is   the   name   our   Native   American
    ancestors
gave to God because they knew
God is mysteriously part of everything
    and everyone
Quiet love
penetrating the depths of eternity from
    one end to the other
birthing us to life
at every moment, day and night.
I believe that Jesus gave birth to God in
    humanity
uniquely as no one else in human history
as movement, as life, as goodness,
as love.
I think of Jesus as the incarnation of
    'quiet love.'

I think, too, of all the people confined to
    silence, not by choice,
in cells of solitude, prisoners of their
    body,
the windows of their minds closed to
    the familiar faces of yesterday.
Quiet love silenced by the slow
    deterioration of the mind
or worse, empty souls, searching for
    someone to love.
And many who have lost their way on
    lonely streets
or in caves of dark despair
waiting for quiet love to free them from
    the isolation of insignificance
or the dysfunction of worthlessness
 or ironically, iconic vanity.
Waiting for quiet love to touch them.
Meanwhile the pundits preach
from pulpits, of their political superiority
a gospel of narcissism to be sure,
spreading their feathers like pheasants
    looking for a mate—and a vote.
And what of the evangelical 'merchants'
    with gold rings

in search of fine pearls instead of tending
lost sheep?

Stealthy 'guardians' of sound doctrine
and dogma,

stern sponsors of stoic rites and rituals,

moved more by fear of the unknown
than by awe of the Mystery;

assuring firm adherence to rules and
rubrics

that harken back to other ages—the dark
ages

lest they be quickened by a new move-
ment of the Spirit

God Spirit.

Yet quiet love seeps through the cracks
and crevices

of ancient times and places

and over time we come to know our
origin

and our destiny

in quiet love—

that will not be silenced.

Dark Spaces

Blue sparkling diamonds
splashed across fields of dark muted
    skies
Winking at ages long past.
Tall naked trees
each with a unique story
not yet penned on hidden clouds.
Silhouetted branches black on black
reaching for the star
their hands joined in prayer.
Soft satin breezes
teasing wooden celebrants in the chilled
    night air,
prodding their dark boned aged fingers
    to play their ancient song
as if to welcome the mystic dawn.

Ah, the true meaning of the feast is
    found not in the light of day
but in the dark spaces between the notes
    of the symphony—
measure by measure interrupted now
    and then
by the sudden blast of nothingness.

Are you listening? It's your song and
    mine
played in the mystic night, soul food—
food for the soul waiting for liberation,
for incarnation, icon of the eternal God
singing God's song in the eternal night
moving toward eternal light—
low tech in a sea of tweet and twitter.

Christmas is for contemplatives, artists
    and poets
who speak the language of the stars
    splashed on stained glass windows
in green backyard cathedrals and street
    churches
in the shadow of lofty canyons of glass
    and steel.

Do not be silent—sing your song
Amidst those who yearn to dance with
    the stars,
rich and poor, lost and found,
in the alleys of ravaged war-torn planets
across generations of the exploited past
and scorching present.
Christ has died,
Christ is risen,
Christ will come again!

In the Light of the Star I Stand

No, I kneel
as I contemplate the mystery unfolding
throughout the ages:
Sophia,
Sapientia,
Wisdom
The God within
that impregnates humanity
in an ever-evolving manifestation
here
there
everywhere.
Angels testified to the unique event—
the Christ event that
caught our attention—briefly;
a reminder of our weakness
of our greatness.
But you say, if this be so
where are the signs in the town square?
in city halls
within the walls of congress
in the homes of governors

in the courts of jurists
on the 'killing fields'
in the stockpiles of weapons.
Whose side is God on anyway?
Theirs, ours?
Mine, yours?

In the light of the star
breadlines of the hungry
on line for the feast that never ends.
Hunger that is never quite satiated,
Thirst that is never quenched.
Is prosperity the entitlement only of the
        affluent—I among them?
And poverty strictly for the poor?

In the light of the star
we move out of the shadow of abun-
        dance
unabashed we see our poverty
not of gilt or gold but
of spirit clothed in empty promises
to lift one another's burdens
to set free the oppressed.

In the light of the star
We come to our senses
In the pulpit and pew—
silent no longer.
Our blindness removed
Our tethered dreams unleashed

In the light of the star
We pray for one another.

Whom shall we invite to the feast this
year?

Season of Gratefulness
And What of Gratitude?

It was a random survey
brief—
no warning—
in no sense scientific, informal.
Your preference, please,
Thanksgiving or Christmas?
A landslide victory for Thanksgiving!
Turkey and the trimmings?
No!
Freshly baked pies: apple and pumpkin?
Not at all!
Then why Thanksgiving over Christmas?
No countdown before the feast.
No trips to the mall.
No presents, only your presence!
A time to be together, no strings
    attached.
Come as you are.
But what of the birth of Jesus?
Did he not make a difference?
Does he not make a difference still?
Indeed, he did; indeed he does.

Jesus is the reason for the season and for
the feast.
But except for a brief pageant in the
parish church,
and a passing nod at the crèche
we are caught up in the heat of the night
rather than the Light that shattered the
darkness of the night.
It occurred to me that giving thanks is all
about tables,
the Jesus-table,
your table and mine
and the table of humanity.
It's about keeping them all connected
Remember?

This brief reflection, the gift of a friend,
expresses it simply but so much more
powerfully
than my feeble attempt at the same:

In the Eucharist, or Lord's Supper,
Jesus gave us something that he did
not say
We needed to 'think about' or 'agree
upon,'

'understand,' 'look at,' or even 'worship.'
Instead, he just said, 'Eat this'
And 'give thanks'　　　　　*(eucharisteo,*
　　　　　　　　　　　　　Luke 22:17)
To the one who gives you bread,
And who is the origin of your own life
　　and goodness.
It is something we do at the cellular level
More than the cerebral level.
Every day we must make a deep choice
for gratitude, abundance ('there is
　　enough')
and appreciation,
which always de-centers the self
and its cravings.
It is the core meaning of worship.
Your life is pure gift,
And it must be based on an attitude of
　　gratitude.

[Adapted from "Things Hidden: Scripture as Spirituality," pp. 215-216, *Everything Belongs*, Richard Rohr, OFM, 2008.]

No 'bah humbug' here...
Just getting reacquainted
With the real meaning of the feast.

Healing Love

Woman wrapped in silence
resting in the cold night
waiting for the sun to rise
and a new day to bring new life.

Woman unknown,
under stars light years away—
under the star destined to shine over all
    the ages.

Waiting woman wrapped in mystery
carrying within her womb the child God,
child unwanted
by earthly gods of gift and gold
of power and prestige
of weapons and war.

Woman wrapped in wisdom—Sophia,
Transparent soul filled with God and
    grace
to bring forth 'Sophia' Son of light.
in whom there is no darkness—
no east or west,
incarnate,

neither male or female—
the Christ,
the same yesterday, today and forever.

Courageous woman called blessed
from generation to generation.
Gentle woman in whom no sin is found.
Woman priest of God brings forth the
    lamb of God
who takes away the sins of the world—
enduring love,
healing lover.

Treasured Moments

To my frequent childhood plea:
"I wish it were—
tomorrow,
the next day,
or Christmas!"
my mother would reply:
"Stop wishing your life away!"

In our relentless rush toward tomorrow
and toward the millennium,
we can overlook too easily
the treasured moments of today
and the people who make our life special
every day.

Though the Feast is indeed coming
    quickly
and soon thereafter the millennium,
God, Emmanuel is always present
wherever kind people extend them-
    selves for others.

I believe that Jesus reflected
the mystery of God's presence in our
    world.

I believe that his relationship with God
can be ours too
and that we can reflect God's goodness
to others in humble but significant ways.

I am grateful over and over
for the many ways
you have shown to me, the face of God
throughout the years.

May you be blessed abundantly
by our generous God
during this season
and in every season.

Season of Promise
A Christmas Prayer

Quare tristis incedo? (Psalm 43:10b)
I promised,
you promised
to be faithful forever
vowed to Christ or Church.
Gift freely given,
gift freely accepted:
single and celibate,
married or partnered,
'in season and out of season'
no fair-weather friendship,
no quid-pro-quo agreement,
no contract necessary,
no signatures other than the imprint of
    the heart
heart-to-heart.
Autographs in the misty sky
on clouds midst stars set deep in sockets
    beyond yesterday
But life changes in time over time.

What appeared real has become surreal
amidst thickened clouds,
stormy weather,
the likes of which no one has ever seen,
or at least can ever recall;
fires, floods and earthquakes
and wars.
Sudden crashes on the highway
innocent life snuffed out in an instant.
No exemptions or exceptions:
women, men and children,
rich and poor,
black, white, brown and yellow
Muslim, Hindu, Buddhist, Jew and
    Christian
all succumbing to forces beyond human
    endurance.
Lilies in the field left to drown.
Sparrows without nests.
Who cares?
But there's more you say.
What of worldly rulers
clothed in red, white and blue
who speak victoriously of justice but
    who act with vengeance?

And of religious chiefs,
"shepherds" they call themselves
but in truth, wolves in sheep's clothing?
Justice is now measured and meted out
 by the unjust.
Legal   cover-ups   reflecting   shallow
 wisdom bereft of moral courage
unworthy compromise on any standard,
 human or divine.
"See I told you," chants the atheist,
"There is no God!"
The agnostic chimes in with meek refrain,
"If God there be, we cannot know for
 sure;"
for this God does not speak or act with
 reverence toward the human
but stands aloof, detached from human-
 kind.
This cannot be you say.
Our promises were not in vain
for God has indeed appeared over time.
Promise fulfilled in time
in place and space
where angels fear to tread.

A noble God who cares not about title
or race, or color
or earthly kin of any kind
whose imprint is on every precious soul
no matter who or how the cause of
being.
Indeed, "I will call this to mind, as my
reason to have hope:
The favors of the Lord are not exhausted,
God's mercies are not spent;
They are renewed each morning so
great is God's faithfulness.
My portion is the Lord, says my soul;
Therefore will I hope in God.
Good is the Lord to the one who waits
for God
to the soul that seeks God.
It is good to hope in silence
for the saving help of the Lord."

(Lamentations 3:21-26)

A New Year's Prayer

Here I am again, Lord,
at the door of another year
of challenge and opportunity;

It seems
I have been down this road before—
more times than I can count.
I confess to you
that I have been less than content with
and more than inept in
the fulfillment of countless promises
spoken and unspoken,
that I have made to you.
I suspect they were not so much for you
    but for me.
Promises make me feel good
as if I have already given something of
    myself.
But in reality,
cotton candy promises that taste sweet
    on contact
but whose taste quickly vanishes;
instantly forgotten.

Somehow,
promises seem to take the pressure off
as if to appease an expectant taskmaster
or demanding parent.
"I promise…"
But I'm not always as good as my
    promises.
I think that perhaps
I need to rethink this whole notion
and substitute instead
an attentive ear to your promise
to me
and to humanity.
I think I may have assumed too much
as if by this time I knew your mind
and what you expect of me.
How silly.
Who can know your mind
or who can fathom your thoughts?
Perhaps this year
I will listen more carefully
and come to know that your expectations
are more realistic than mine.
Perhaps this year
I will also come to know

that your promise is more important
than mine
and in fact that it has been fulfilled
in the Christ
and continues to be fulfilled
each time that I say "yes, Lord,
I believe;
help my unbelief."
The New Year is less about our promises
as it is about learning to breathe the air
that Jesus breathed;
to inhale the "Spirit"
that Jesus lived.
Only by listening
as did Mary
not so much with our ears
as with our hearts
can we hear what God is asking of us
this year.
I suspect we already know.

Season of Joy
May I Have This Dance?

Music was in the air
and in our veins;
Dancing in our DNA.
We danced in the ballroom
and danced in the backyard;
we danced in grandma's basement too.
Mom and dad were first up on the dance
    floor
and the last to sit down.
And you know what?
We couldn't tell who was leading whom.
They were best friends as well as lovers.
I reckon that's the secret of a lifelong
    relationship.
All creation is a dance.
And there's a dance in every person.
And there's a dance for every season.
All that is needed is a bit of soul
and music in the air!
Does God dance?
I think so.
The great mystics old and new say so:

"Whatever is going on in God is a flow,
a radical relationship, a perfect com-
    munion
between three, a circle dance of love."
    (Richard Rohr)
We are invited to participate; to be
    partners
in the divine dance
or rather, to recognize that we are
    already in the circle
In the flow of the Trinitarian dance;
mutual love of Father/Mother and Son/
    Sophia;
a generative love that embraces all
    creation
through the grace of the Holy Spirit.
Those who live the rhythm of God
swim in the sea of God's grace.
A metaphor, to be sure,
But how better to express divine love
pulsating throughout the ages in space
    and time,
in the galaxies, cosmic storms and
    supernovas,

in the sun, in the moon and stars light
   years away.
I think this is what we celebrate at
   Christmas.
Will you dance with me this Christmas?
I wish you all the graces and blessings of
   this season
and of every season.

Season of Memories
Shadows

We continue to live
in the shadow of towers
that are no longer.
The mind plays tricks
as if history could be rewound—
a video tape
and DVD
back to the beginning
a new start.
Distraught memories deleted.
Wounds   healed   before   they   were
    inflicted—
erasable disk
CD rom—permanently disabled
buried deep among the fragments of
    ages past,
archetypes of another time and place.

We have lived more recently
in the shadow of other towers
not of steel or stone
vessels of clay

shattered images
men in white robes
consecrated to holiness,
inflated,
desecrated by desires unholy,
unfettered,
stained windows.

Can we not dismantle the remnant of
    these towers too
as if to make believe they never fell?
Or shall we simply say:
"We are sorry?"
and promise "that it won't happen
    again?"

But life cannot be erased
or tortured memories deleted.

The template can be changed
but the image remains deeply imbedded
in the minds and hearts of those who
    trusted too much.

We survive despite ungodly forces
outside our walls

and within our walls.
Indeed, wolves in sheep's clothing near
and far
that impinge upon our sacred space
threatening to rob our souls of innocence
and our urge to revenge.

But should not life be more than
survival?
The dye has not been cast forever.

No barren branch or empty vine.
Are we bereft of life or hope?
Incarnational seed sown in fertile soil.
Stem of Jesse
rooted in goodness—
Godliness.

"I will call this to mind,
as my reason to have hope:
the favors of the Lord are not exhausted.
God's mercies are not spent;
they are renewed each morning,
so great is God's faithfulness.
Let us reach out our hearts toward God
in heaven." (Lamentations 3:17-26, 41)

The Time Trap

Quiet clouds moving slowly over the
   crest of yesterday,
dismissing time as if in the eternal
   present
where life and death meet
neither fearing the other.
The echoes of ancient carols still sound
   in the distance;
the days of merry-making almost spent
yet not giving way to tomorrow
'til new memories are safely tucked
   away for another day—
for another year, next year and the next
Quests pursued unfinished, questions
   still remain
in a dense fog that never ends
against the background of the dark forest
   without trees.
Preachers and politicians ascend their
   bully pulpits
speaking a language they do not
   understand—
lacking depth in mind and heart,

empty speech devoid of guilt or spirit;
congregants cheer the hollow words
   with silence.
Soon we must wake to a new day—
the beginning of a new story,
a new gospel, good news,
better news
of truth, not fiction or fable,
a new myth that hints at the unexplained
   mystery
hidden in the depth of my soul for
   centuries
yearning to be recognized
to be set free
ready and willing to free prisoners of
   darkness
tearing down walls of prickly thoughts.
Tomorrow will come, ready or not, like
   it or not
and with it the untold story unfolding in
   the town square—
in Times Square.
The crystal ball descends from among
   the stars
withholding the future,

searching for someone to listen to
   tomorrow
where quiet voices have been waiting
to speak good news to those caught in
   the trap of time—
the time trap.
who are they?
Black, white and brown,
single and partnered,
straight and gay,
rich and poor,
liberal and conservative,
special needs,
no needs.
You? Me?
Tomorrow is waiting for us all.
So come to the table!
Bridge-builders welcomed
where life begins and ends.
Where truth unfolds,
where differences fade,
giving in to the heartbeat of a higher
   truth,
not yours, or mine.
God's truth.

Are you listening?
Stay awake!
The clouds are passing.
The fog is lifting.
The forest has turned to green again.
The mystery unfolds.
The eternal presence is now.
Come let us break the bread of ancient
    wisdom
of emerging poets and prophets.
Be not anxious for tomorrow.
Put to rest the restless and unruly
    thoughts of yesterday.
Times change and we change with them.
No trap, only the passing of time.
May you be blessed with the grace and
    blessings
of this season and of every season.
Jesus Christ is the same yesterday, today
    and forever!

Season of Truth
Ultimate Truth

"I will hear what God proclaims,
the Lord—for he proclaims peace
to his people and to his faithful ones
and to those who put in him their hope.

"Near indeed is his salvation
to those who reverence him,
glory dwelling in our land.

"Mercy and truth shall meet;
justice and peace shall embrace.
Truth shall spring out of the earth
And justice shall look down from the
    heavens.

"Justice shall walk before him,
and salvation along the way of his steps."
    (Psalm 85)

It has been said by someone that
"Truth has a thousand faces."
Indeed!

But there is an ultimate truth
unmasked, pure, without cunning or
    craftiness
or face-saving prolixity.
And there is justice in the heart of God—
unmitigated,
equal treatment for all under the law of
    God.

There is no mercy without truth
and no peace without justice.

May truth and mercy meet
and may justice and peace embrace
that we may all experience
the saving power of God in Christ
during this season
and every season.

Again, As If for the First Time

It has been said
more than once that
only prophets and poets speak
"the truth,
the whole truth
and nothing but the truth."
But what is truth?
And how do we recognize truth
when so many lay claim to it.
I suspect, however, it may be more a
    question
of who is prophet or poet
and who is not.
Who are they who dare lay claim
to clairvoyant understanding of the
    movement of God
in the affairs of men and women
when in this life of trial and travail
we see only glimpses of truth through
    reflections?
Broken mirrors—
shattered glass upon the grass.
Remnants of visions rejected;
windows "stained" in mud
telling stories that belie the madness of
    dreams turned nightmares,

mythic heroes refashioned into reality
history revised to shape our thinking
    into just war theories,
refurbished slices of the past.
No poets and prophets allowed here.
"We stand for peace not war!"
The less moral in the face of the immoral.
Our case and cause take precedence in
    the face of violence,
threats of mass destruction
making life ambiguous
and making us ambivalent about poets
    and prophets
soothsayers with swords of peace,
words that shatter visions of imminent
    victory.
Indeed, war doth make enemies of
    friends and lovers
and of enemies, strange bedfellows.
Perhaps to truth itself we would prefer
    contentment.
Though we continue to celebrate the
    birth of the Savior
we remain 'Easter people'
who continue to expect the unexpected
to happen again as if
for the first time.

On this day of new beginnings
we think especially of those who have
    no alternative
but to start over again—
from scratch
in the face of the brutal attack of nature.
None of us will get out of life alive
or will we?
Do we dare hope that our life in Christ
will or can sustain us in the face of the
    most wicked forces
even death itself?
The outpouring of help to the poorest of
    the poor
throughout the world
in India and Indonesia and every island
    in between
is more than a ray of hope
that Christ who came once
has come again;
Christ who died
has risen again.
Perhaps it will be true again this year
as true as it was the first time.

Postscript

Were it not for Christmas
would we take the time
and the space
to be reminded
how much we mean to one another?
And would we stop and think about the
    one
who makes our life fruitful?

Lord,
Bless those who add such a beautiful
    dimension to life—
who care so deeply
about the happiness of others.
Their generosity is surpassed
only by your infinite love.

May the birth of the Christ make us
    thankful
and continue to make a difference in our
    lives.